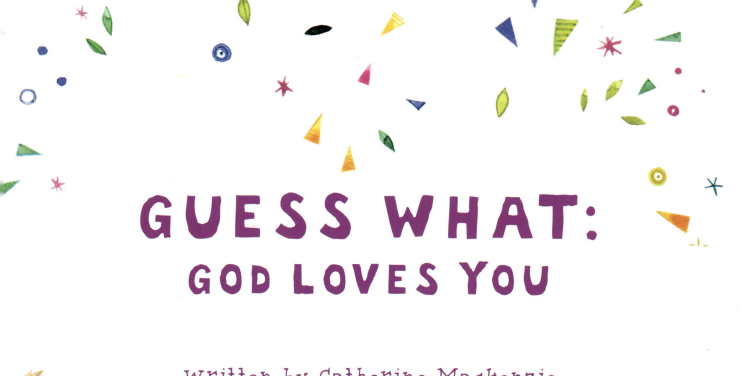

GUESS WHAT:
GOD LOVES YOU

written by Catherine Mackenzie
Illustrated by Ola Krzanowska

CF4KIDS

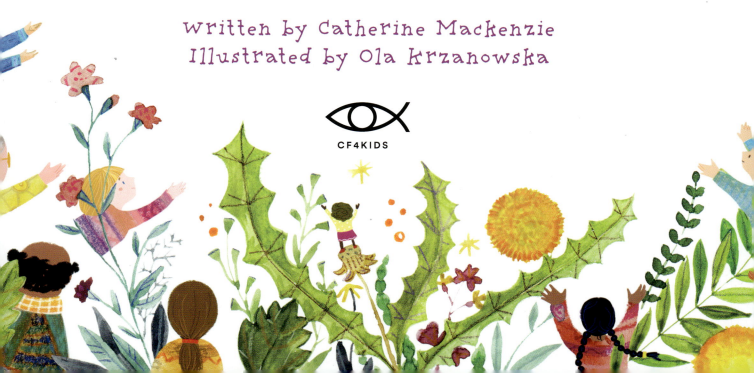

Guess what! God loves you!

Does he love you more than sparrows? Yes! You are worth more than many sparrows.

(Matthew 10:29-31)

Guess what! God loves you!

Does he love you more than lilies? Definitely. God clothes flowers like kings. He'll clothe you better.
(Luke 12:27-28)

Guess what! God loves you!

Does he love you more than comfort? For sure. When Jesus came to live on earth he was poor. Life was hard. He was tired, hungry and sometimes sad. He did that for you!

(Matthew 8:20)

Guess what! God loves you!

Does God love you more than life? Absolutely.
God's Son, Jesus, died to save sinful people
from the wrong things we do.
Our sin does not please God,
but it does not stop God from loving us.
While we were still sinners Jesus died for us.
If you love God it is because God loved you first.
He loves you most. He loves you best!

(1 John 4:19; Romans 5:8)

Guess what! God loves you!

God's love is so great that nothing can keep you apart from it.

God will work out everything for good if you trust in him. Not even something as sad as death can stop God's good plans for you. God's power burst Jesus out of the grave.

(Romans 8:28)

Guess what! God loves you!

Nothing at all can keep you apart from God's love.

Nothing that is alive. Nothing that is dead.

Nothing in the past or in the future!

Nothing in today and nothing in tomorrow.

Nothing bad and nothing powerful can keep God from loving you. Nothing up high and nothing down low.

(Psalm 103:11)

Nothing in the sky.

Nothing under the sky.

Nothing under the ocean.

If you trust in Jesus, not one thing can keep you apart from God's love. Your troubles can't trick him. Hardships won't halt him. Dangers can't deter him. You can trust him completely!

Jesus is God's love.
Trust in him.

Guess what! God loves you!

Not even death, nor life, nor angels nor rulers, nor things present nor things to come, nor powers, nor height nor depth, nor anything else in all creation, will be able to separate us from the love of God in Christ Jesus our Lord.

(Romans 8:38-39)

Christian Focus is for Kids

That means you and your friends can all find a book to help you from the CF4KIDS range – from the very littlest baby to kids that are almost too old to be called a kid anymore.
We publish books that introduce you to the real Jesus, the truth of God's Word, and what that means for boys and girls of all ages.
Reading books is a fun way to find out what it is like to be a follower of Jesus Christ. True stories, adventures, activity books, and devotions – they are all here for you and your family.
Christian Focus is part of the family of God. We aim to glorify Jesus and help you trust and follow Him.

Christian Focus Publications Ltd,
Geanies House, Fearn, Ross-shire, IV20 1TW, Scotland,
United Kingdom.
www.christianfocus.com

Author's Dedication:
Many thanks to two individuals who really helped me think through this concept of the love of God and the promises of God: my pastor John Ferguson and my friend Connie Dever.

10 9 8 7 6 5 4 3 2 1
Copyright © 2025 Catherine MacKenzie
ISBN:978-1-5271-1197-4
Published by Christian Focus Publications,
Geanies House, Fearn, Tain, Ross-shire, IV20 1TW, U.K.
Illustrations by Ola Krzanowska
Printed and bound by Gutenberg, Malta

All rights reserved. No part of this publication may be reproduced, stored in a retrieval system, or transmitted, in any form, by any means, electronic, mechanical, photocopying, recording or otherwise without the prior permission of the publisher or a licence permitting restricted copying. In the U.K. such licences are issued by the Copyright Licensing Agency, 4 Battlebridge Lane, London, SE1 2HX. www.cla.co.uk